A Breath of Kindness

EXPRESSIONS OF FRIENDSHIP

A GIFT FOR

_____

FROM

_____

A Breath
of Kindness

Artwork copyright © 2002 ROYAL DOULTON
Royal Doulton® is a trademark. Used under
license by DaySpring Cards, Inc.

Text copyright ©2002 DaySpring Cards, Inc.

Published by Garborg's™,
a brand of DaySpring Cards, Inc.
Siloam Springs, Arkansas

Design by Garborg Design Works

Compiled by Vicki P. Graham
Edited by Mary Hollingsworth

ISBN 1-58061-361-6

Printed in China

A Breath of Kindness

EXPRESSIONS OF FRIENDSHIP

A Breath of Kindness

Expressions of Friendship

GARBORG'S

Introduction

For nearly two hundred years Royal
Doulton has attracted the best craftsmen
and artists in the industry, producing
the highest quality bone china. Now
their elegant patterns are paired with
expressions of friendship in an offering
that blends the unparalleled beauty of
inspirational verse with the lasting
inspiration of beautiful art and design.

On the instant of meeting after a long separation and with no sense of a time lapse, to rediscover an easy and comfortable relationship—this is one of the joys of friendship.

Henry Dreyfuss

The Breath of Kindness

Oh, the comfort—the

    Inexpressible comfort of

    Feeling safe with a person.

Having neither to weigh thoughts,

Nor measure words, but

    Pouring them

All right out, just as

    They are—

Chaff and grain together—

Certain that a faithful

Hand will

Take and sift them,

Keep what is worth

Keeping,

And with the breath of

Kindness

Blow the rest away.

Dinah Maria Mulock Craik

The Friend Who Just Stands By

When trouble comes your soul to try,

You love the friend who just "stands by."

Perhaps, there's nothing he can do—

The thing is strictly up to you;

For there are troubles all your own,

And paths the soul must tread alone;

Times when love cannot smooth the road

Nor friendship lift the heavy load,

But just to know you have a friend

Who will "stand by" until the end,

Whose sympathy through all endures,

Whose warm handclasp is always yours—

It helps, someway, to pull you through,

Although there's nothing he can do.

And so with fervent heart you cry,

"God bless the friend who just 'stands by'!"

B. Y. Williams

It's the friends you can call up at 4 a.m.
that matter.

Marlene Dietrich

Friends share

all things.

PYTHAGORAS

Implicit in the bond of friendship is the
understanding that whatever befalls you is
important to me—but we need never say so.

Chet Huntley

Standing By Your Heart

You call me friend...

But do you realize

How much the name implies...

It means that down the years,

Through sunshine and through tears,

There's always someone standing by your

Heart.

You call me friend...

And thus your life and mine

Grow richer in design...

And I would have you know,

Wherever you may go,

There's always someone standing by your

Heart.

Hilda Butler Farr

Wishes for My Friend

I wish I could take away your pain and sorrow, heap them up and blow them away. I wish I could give you the successes and loves and peace for which you long. I wish I could take from my happiness and patch the holes in yours.

If I can share your burdens and your
achievements, they'll be twice as light
and twice as wonderful. And maybe
that will make up for my not being able
to give you your world.

V. Graham

What Made

What made us

Friends in the long ago

When first we met?

Well, I think I know:

The best in me

And the best in you

Hailed each other

Because they knew

Us Friends?

That always and always

Since life began

Our being friends

Was part of God's plan.

George Webster Douglas

Yes, we must ever be friends;

and of all who offer you friendship

Let me be ever the first, the truest,

the nearest and the dearest!

Longfellow

There are moments in life when all that we can bear is the sense that our friend is near us; our wounds would wince at the touch of consoling words that would reveal the depths of our pain.

Honoré de Balzac

He loseth keepeth God

I will not leave you comfortless. I will come back to you.

The Book of John

*nothing that
for his friend.*

THOMAS FULLER

Thank God for friends, more prized as years

    Increase.

Let all else, if must be, cease.

But, Lord of Life, I pray on me bestow

    The gift of friends

To share the way I go.

Thomas Curtis Clark

Flowers are lovely; love is flower-like;

Friendship is a sheltering tree;

Oh, the joys that come down shower-like!

Samuel Taylor Coleridge

Heaven Half Begun

For once or twice within a lifetime, we

Find someone whom we love

    For that which is

Dependent not on looks or qualities…

Call it soul, spirit, personality…

The thing which is no other but that one,

The thing which will not die

    When life is done.

And that we join to us in such a way

That neither fate nor change

    Nor ill repute

Can ever grow so strong as to refute

The bond, nor time bring any least decay...

Friendship like this, if life

    Holds only one

Is well lived and heaven half begun.

Florence B. Jacobs

Love fulfills our need to be
sympathetically understood by
someone to whom we can pour out
our troubles, by whom we can be
comforted, and with whom we can go
on to find gladness.

F. Alexander Magoun

What helps us in friendship is not so much the help our friends give us as the assurance that they *will* help.

Epicurus

The Blessings

There are friends who are to us like a great rock in a weary land. We flee to them in the heat of parching days and rest in their shadow. A friend in whom we can confide without fear of disappointment; who, we are sure, will never fail us, will never stint his love in serving us, who always has

of Friendship

healing tenderness of the hurt of our
heart, comfort for our sorrow, and cheer
for our discouragement, such a friend is
not only a rock of shelter to us in time of
danger, but is also as rivers of water in a
thirsty land, when our hearts cry out for
life and love.

J. R. Miller

Because of You

What if I reach the end of my lifeline

Without telling you how much you

 mean to me?

What if something happens and I haven't

 told you

That the best of times were and are

 ever sweeter

Because you're here to share my joy?

What if I haven't told you that your

 holding my hand

Through the saddest and most

 poignant times

Enabled me to hold my head high

And walk right through those

  darkest hours.

I pray God to let my pen speak

  where my lips cannot.

I want you to know you are a treasure

  in my life,

Your jewels of love and friendship

  through thick and thin

Are priceless, and my lifetime is

  brighter and richer

Because you're part of it.

Simply, I love you, and I appreciate you.

There, now I've said it!

V. Graham

I Want To Be Your Friend

Fluent with a friend,

The only word unspoken

Is *sayonara*.

Traditional

I want to be your friend

Forever and ever without break or decay.

When the hills are all flat

And the rivers are all dry,

When it lightnings and thunders in winter,

When it rains and snows in summer,

When leaves and earth mingle—

Not till then will I part from you.

First Century Chinese

Friendship

A rendezvous

   Which two hearts keep

Beyond

   All time, aware

In joy or sorrow

   One may come

And find the other

   There.

Mary Wheeler Edgerton

Eloquent Silence

We don't always have to talk, and
I'm glad we're comfortable being quiet
together. I draw incredible strength and
hope by just being in the same room
with you or walking with you through
a quiet park. The silence between us
says so many things eloquently. It says,

"I trust you to understand my mood today." "I'm thankful I don't need to try and impress you with my words." "I love you, and you know it without my always having to say so." "I need to be with you today—just be with you."

If you must say something to me today, say it with a smile, a hug, or a squeeze of my hand. I'll understand. Some things are better said with silence.

Mary Hollingsworth

A friend is one
about you and
the same.

Love is blind;

Friendship closes its eyes.

French Proverb

My friend is not perfect, and neither am I...we suit each other quite well.

who knows all

loves you just

Always

You've always been there and known at
a glance or by my voice what I needed.
You've always said exactly what I
wanted to hear, a word of kindness and
encouragement, advice from the heart,
or just "I love you." You've always
made me believe everything would be
all right and given me the courage, not
to *plod* on, but to *run* on. (And maybe,

as I look back, you didn't even believe it yourself.) You've never laughed at my dreams, and you've helped me to realize some of them, and reminded me of others long forgotten. You've always prompted me to follow my heart and to trust its goodness. I am a better person because of you.

V. Graham

Of all the blossoms in friendship's garden, kindness is the most fragrant.

A friend you give

is a present
yourself.

A friend is someone you like because
you like yourself better in his company.

Two people are better than one. When two people work together, they get more from the work they do. If one person falls, then the other person can help him up. But it is very bad for the person that is alone when he falls; there is no one there to help him....

An enemy might be able to defeat one person, but that enemy can't defeat two people. And three people are even stronger. They are like a rope that has three parts wrapped together—it is very hard to break.

The Book of Ecclesiastes

A friend sings your song when you forget the words.

Friendship

There is something in your friendship

    Very sweet for rainy days—

'Tis your thoughtfulness in finding

    What I like in little ways,

And of doing one by one,

    Things that others leave undone.

There is something in your friendship
    Sane and strong and glad and true,
Which makes better worth the doing
    Everything I have to do,
And your friendly word and smile
    Somehow helps make life worthwhile.

There is something in your friendship
    Very rare to find, my friend,
'Tis unselfishness in giving
    Without stint and without end;
So there is—at last I learn—
    Love that asks for no return.

There is something in your friendship
That has stood through many a test,
Giving me a sense of safety,
Of security and rest—
Friend of mine, my whole life through,
I am glad that I met you.

"Ideals" Magazine

In the multitude of my anxious
thoughts within me, your comfort
cheers and delights my soul.

The Book of Psalms

The friend given you by circumstances
over which you have no control was
God's own gift.

Frederick Robertson

Friendship
is Love
without
his wings.

LORD BYRON

The ornament
the friends who

A true friend is one who comes to your
house and makes *you* feel at home.

f a house is frequent it.

RALPH WALDO EMERSON

Some people come into our lives and
quickly leave, while some stay awhile
leaving footprints on our hearts, and
we are never the same again.

True friendship
comes when
the silence
between two
people is
comfortable.

My Book,

I cherish visits with you as I cherish reading a good book. I set special time aside for just me and my book, and I can't wait to get into its pages, to pick up where I left off, to escape the real world for awhile.

That's the way we are; no bother with niceties of reacquaintance and politeness. We simply dig into our own dramas and let the conversation flow, much like turning the pages as fast as we can.

My Friend

My book is exciting, and sad, and funny, and oftentimes maddening. And I can't bear to put it down. It's the same with our times together. The pages fly by as we fill ourselves with the stuff of our lives. And, like a good book that I reluctantly put down when responsibility calls, I reluctantly part from you, part from our escape together...till another time.

V. Graham

May your love be

unfailing
my comfort.

Old friends are best. King James used
to call for his old shoes; they were
easiest for his feet.

John Selden

Comfortably Together

My coat and I live comfortably together. It has assumed all my wrinkles, does not hurt me anywhere, has molded itself to my deformities and is complacent to all my movements. I only feel its presence because it keeps me warm. Old coats and old friends are the same.

Victor Hugo

*Friendship
is love
with
kindness.*

Life is like a great ship with room
aboard for many people. Friends who
hop on and off, charming but quickly
forgotten. Friends who sail along when
all is placid, adding pleasure to the trip.
And those friends whom you can
depend on, fair weather or foul;

who will ride out the very worst storms
with you and see you safely to port. I
love this spacious and sturdy vessel
and christened it long ago: My ship of
friends—the FRIENDSHIP.

Marjorie Holmes

There is nothing we like to see so much as the gleam of pleasure in our friend's eye when she feels that we have sympathized with her.

A Mile

O who will walk a mile with me

Along life's merry way?

A comrade blithe and full of glee

Who dares to laugh out loud and free,

And let his frolic fancy play,

with Me

Like a happy child, through the flowers gay

That fill the field and fringe the way

Where he walks a mile with me.

And who will walk a mile with me

Along life's weary way?

A friend whose heart has eyes to see

The stars shine out o'er the darkening lea,

And the quiet rest at the end o' the day—

A friend who knows, and dares to say,

The brave, sweet words that cheer the way

Where he walks a mile with me.

With such a comrade, such a friend,

I fain would walk till journey's end,

Through summer sunshine, winter rain,

And then?

Farewell, we shall meet again!

Henry Van Dyke

Fate chooses our relatives;

we choose our friends.

Jacques Delille

Without friends no one would

choose to live, though he had

all other goods.

Aristotle

Friendship and Kindness walk arm-in-arm through life. One without the other is bittersweet; together they are joy and comfort. For one is silver, the other gold.

To A Young Friend

Your hair is golden…

Mine turning gray,

Yet we two are walking

The same highway,

You just beginning…

I, near the end,

But what does age matter

When choosing a friend?

Freedom

There can be no friendship
where there is no freedom. Thank you
for that liberating gift. Thank you for
allowing me to speak freely, and act so,
too, and for keeping your mouth shut
when I should not have opened mine.
Thank you for not penning me up in
straight-and-narrow enclosures,

and for being there when I should have set my own boundaries. Thank you for encouraging me and believing in me even when you didn't agree with me. Thank you for that free air we have with each other, an atmosphere called Friendship.

V. Graham

No medicine is more valuable, none
more efficacious, none better suited
to the cure of all our temporal ills
than a friend to whom we may turn
for consolation in time of troubles,
and with whom we may share our
happiness in time of joy.

Saint Ailred of Rievaulx

Heaven comes down to touch us when
we find ourselves safe in the heart of
another person.

For the Love

O, for the love of a friend whose voice and touch will rainbow sorrows, diamond tears, making of them gems of rarest joy: one who forgives all my shortages ere asked to do so; one who dares to the uttermost of human imagery; one whose ship will cast anchor, and throw out the lifeline of hope when storms are near; one who forgives in me all that I can forgive in myself.

of a Friend

O, for the love of a friend who can be made the sacred trustee of my heart; one who is more to me than the closest relative, one whose very name is so sacred that I want to whisper it softly; one who lingers near my door in time of distress, and stretches forth his hand, which is not empty or cold, and who says little, but feels largely.

Mae Lawson

Make Me Worthy

Since it has been my lot to find...

At every parting of the road...

The helping hand of comrade kind...

To help me with my heavy load...

And since I have no gold to give...

And love alone must make amends...

My humble prayer is while I live...

"God make me worthy of my friends."

To a Friend

You entered my life in a casual way,

    And saw at a glance what I needed;

There were others who passed me or

met me each day,

    But never a one of them heeded.

Perhaps you were thinking of other

folks more,

Or chance simply seemed to decree it;

I know there were many such chances

before,

   But the others—well, they didn't see it....

There are times when encouragement means such a lot;

And a word is enough to convey it;
There were others who could have, easy as not—

But, just the same, they didn't say it....

You helped me refashion the dreams of my heart,

And made me turn eagerly to it;
There were others who might have (I question that part)—

But, after all, they didn't do it!

Grace Stricker Dawson

Thank you, my friend, for your love
and kindness. Your friendship is my
special treasure, always caring, never
failing.